WHY ARE YOU HERE?

WHY ARE YOU HERE?

FRANK J. PETER

LUMINARE PRESS
WWW.LUMINAREPRESS.COM

Why Are You Here?
Copyright © 2023 by Frank J. Peter

All rights reserved. This book or any portion thereof may not be reproduced or used in any manner whatsoever without the express written permission of the publisher, except for the use of brief quotations in a book review.

Printed in the United States of America

Luminare Press
442 Charnelton St.
Eugene, OR 97401
www.luminarepress.com

LCCN: 2023900025
ISBN: 979-8-88679-090-0

*Dedicated to family, friends, and fellow travelers
who have taught me so many priceless lessons
in gratitude, patience, kindness, generosity,
forgiveness, courage, and love along the way.*

Table of Contents

Introduction	1
Why Are You Here?	3
The Lottery	9
The Pursuit of Happiness	11
Reality Check	27
Ode to Freedom	32
Decisions, Decisions, Decisions	38
Self-Cultivation	44
What is Success?	56
Autonomy & Community	69
Finding Yourself	78
Dos & Don'ts	83
Beyond Thanksgiving	98
Integrity & Authenticity	102
Maturity	120
The Power of Words	128
Family, Friends, & Lovers	135
Parenthood	145
The Dignity of Work	162

Influence	169
Just Say Yes	179
The Courage to Be	189
Tick-Tock, Tick-Tock	205
Meditations on Faith	216
The Power of Love	232
A Good Death	246

INTRODUCTION

What you are about to read are the earnest expressions of a serious student of life—someone who has been brought to tears by Pol Pot's killing fields and Beethoven's "Ode to Joy"—and whose firsthand experiences have earned him the right and demand of him the responsibility to speak.

These pages are at once a proclamation of gratitude, an aspiration to become a better person, a celebration of human dignity and potential, an embrace of freedom and responsibility, an appeal for global solidarity and peace, and an invitation to live a deeply-examined and meaningful life.

Every word here began as an honest but not always successful attempt to define and solve my problems of daily existence. Born of confusion, anger, fear, resentment, frustration, shame, despair, illness, heartbreak, regret, and loneliness over the course of decades, these writings took shape from tentative smatterings on scraps of paper to where they are today—still incomplete and still containing more questions than answers—but hopefully a few steps closer to understanding and navigating this mysterious journey called life, with all its sufferings, joys, perils, and possibilities.

But before we begin, a confession is in order. Although I declare many things here with unapologetic enthusiasm and conviction, I am no saint. While I do my best to align my behavior with my core values and transform my rants into meaningful action, I fail in many ways, big and small, almost every day. Please forgive my imperfections and walk with me for a while.

WHY ARE YOU HERE?

You did not choose to be here. Neither were you cast here against your will. You were born before you *had* any will. And you do not yet know when or how your existence will end—by disease, accident, disaster, homicide, suicide, or euthanasia—but that day *will* come. What shall you do in the meantime?

To be clear, the question that confronts you is not "What is the meaning of life?" Neither is the proper question "Why are *we* here?" The question that confronts you is "Why are *you* here." What shall be the meaning of *your* life?

It's not your job—or even your business—to answer the eternal question on behalf of all living creatures. It's enough of a challenge and responsibility to answer the question *of* yourself *for* yourself.

Nobody else—no matter how learned, clever, or wise—can tell you why you are here. That is something you're going to have to work out for yourself.

No matter how impeccable your logic, and no matter how clever your arguments, you will never be able to *reason* your way to a meaningful life.

"Why are you here?"

A question you should ask yourself every morning with such sincerity, intensity, and urgency that it hurts.

"Why are you here?"

Answering this question is never optional. No matter *if* and no matter *how* you ask the question, you answer it with everything you do or fail to do each and every day.

THE LOTTERY

We live on a planet where, every day, thousands of innocent newborns are thrust, purely by accident of birth, into circumstances not of their choosing—segregated into the healthy and not, wealthy and not, beautiful and not, gifted and not, sheltered and not, privileged and not, and everything in between.

We live on a planet where millions of human beings, through no fault of their own, have no hope of enjoying the many conveniences and opportunities that other millions take for granted; where millions would trade everything they own to have the scraps of food that other millions routinely throw away; where millions are condemned to preventable poverty, disease, and violence while millions of others bask in comfort, safety, and luxury.

And here you are, uniquely blessed and burdened, living somewhere between poverty and affluence and somewhere between helplessness and omnipotence. Struggling to find meaning, peace, and happiness somewhere between self-indulgence and self-sacrifice—and never sure that you are doing the right thing, no matter how honorable, generous, and courageous your actions might be.

THE PURSUIT OF HAPPINESS

Physical and mental health. Self-reliance. Freedom from want and freedom from fear. Simple pleasures. Satisfaction of a job well done. Sincere affection. A tender moment. Making love. Mutual respect, trust, and loyalty. A true friend. Meaningful work and carefree play. Communion with nature and communion with others. Teamwork and a sense of belonging. A gift given. A gift received. A problem solved. A lesson learned. A skill mastered. A talent shared. A mistake owned. A destructive habit broken. Self-discovery and self-possession. A mountain climbed. A dream fulfilled. A thrilling experience. An exciting discovery. A golden opportunity. A precious keepsake. A pleasant memory. An inspiring creation. A strong and gentle child raised. A deep sense of gratitude. A simple act of kindness. A wound healed. A promise kept. Justice restored. Abundance shared. Freedom to love as you choose. A hardship endured. An ordeal survived. A clear conscience. Clarity of purpose. Hope for the future. A noble gesture. Service to others. Playing, dancing, singing, laughing, and crying together.

Such are the ingredients of a life well lived.

It is not mere happiness, but meaning that you seek, and the inner peace that comes with a clear conscience.

Happiness—sometimes chosen, sometimes earned, sometimes created, sometimes stumbled upon, sometimes a "reward" for doing the right thing.

Sometimes.

Happiness—so eagerly pursued before we even know what it means. So often unrecognized and unappreciated until we've lost it.

You are unlikely to find meaning, peace, or happiness in obedience, conformity, materialism, dominance, submission, self-indulgence, pragmatism, monasticism, or martyrdom.

You are unlikely to find meaning, peace, or happiness by being "better" than others—by beating them at sports and games, by passing them on the career ladder, by possessing fancier stuff, by having the last word.

It's okay to enjoy life. Enjoyment, done right, is a form of loving yourself and a form of gratitude for the pleasures the universe has to offer—so long as those pleasures are not too guilty—that is, savored without gluttony and never indulged at the expense of others.

How can anyone possibly be content with being content?

How can anyone feel happy "living the good life" unless oblivious to or unmoved by the plight of those less fortunate?

Meaning, peace, and happiness—a never-ending quest to close the gap between who you are and who you aspire to be.

Happiness is like a mirage. Once you "get there," you realize that there is no "there."

Meaning, peace, and happiness—often found in the most "ordinary" things: doing the dishes, a warm hug, a genuine smile, petting the dog next door, a thank you for a kindness you can never repay.

Meaning, peace, and happiness—impossible to find without gratitude, courage, responsibility, empathy, and the acceptance of the things you cannot change.

Meaning, peace, and happiness—sometimes found in leaving a legacy, the projection of hope into a future you will never know and never enjoy.

You, and only you, can judge what meaning, peace, and happiness are made of—given *your* unique endowment of blessings, burdens, passions, and time.

REALITY CHECK

Reality is not just the objective state of what *is*. Reality is the frustrating and painful gap between what *is* and how you wish things would *be*.

Reality is a universe where:

bad things happen to good people,
the greedy prosper and the innocent suffer,
sincere prayers go unanswered,
no good deed goes unpunished,
love does not conquer all,
and some crosses *are* too much to bear.

Reality is unrequited love, lessons learned too late, shattered dreams, lost hope, and holes in your heart that no amount of time will heal.

Reality, sometimes so unforgiving that, no matter how sincere your remorse, you do not get a second chance.

Reality, sometimes so cruel—natural evils so indiscriminate, humans so inhumane—that there is no moral to the story.

Reality—that frustrating and painful gap between what *is* and how we wish things would *be*—is where the most meaningful lives are lived.

ODE TO FREEDOM

No matter how you ask the question about the meaning of your existence, the mere suggestion that life *can* mean something gives birth to an idea that's as terrible as it is wonderful: a thing called *freedom*.

Freedom is not a choice. Freedom just *is*. And no "authority," earthly or divine, can relieve you of this inescapable and never-ending burden.

Freedom lives or dies with everything you do, or fail to do, each and every day.

Refuse to be a mere effect in an indifferent and deterministic universe.

Commit yourself to freedom because without it, all talk of character, virtue, ethics, and love is nonsense.

Commit yourself to freedom because every attempt to escape from freedom will cause you pain.

DECISIONS, DECISIONS, DECISIONS

You become most interesting in those precious, burdensome moments when you decide that you have choices.

You will never have enough time, energy, or means to do everything you would like to do. You must choose—often sacrificing one good for the sake of another. And so, life is the never-ending burden of giving up the things you care about less for the things you care about more.

The first decision you must make is which decisions belong to *you* and which decisions do not.

Sometimes life is so unkind that there is no *good* answer, so frustrating that there is no *right* answer.

There are no *answers* in life, only *choices*. And as the years go by, even in the full light of retrospect, you still may never know if you've chosen wisely.

Easy decisions will continue to seem *hard* with each passing day that you continue to ignore your mortality.

SELF-CULTIVATION

Ignorance may be bliss for some, but don't allow ignorance to become bliss for you.

Truths are many and are not typically pleasant or beautiful. Welcome them anyway. Actively seek them out. Embrace them even when they hurt. Allow them to liberate and empower you by dissolving your ignorance and preconceptions.

Be a student of the entire world, not just the bubble you were born to. Seek knowledge and wisdom from the sacred and secular, conservative and liberal, masculine and feminine, ancient and modern, eastern and western, mainstream and fringe.

Learn how your brain works. Survey the world's religions. Commune with nature. Venture to foreign lands. Get to know people who are different than you. Do honorable things that scare you.

Educate yourself in the liberal arts and in the methods of science. Doing so will inoculate you from self-deception—and also from being deceived by others.

Learn to direct your own attention. Doing so is like a superpower in a world full of hypnotic distractions expertly designed to separate you from your heart, mind, and hard-earned money.

Direct contact with the circumstances of your fellow creatures will teach you more about life than all the philosophy ever written.

Keep your worldview forever open to revision as new evidence and moral arguments present themselves. And dedicate yourself forever to the truth, no matter how inconvenient or humbling that truth might be.

The words of others can steer you down many blind alleys, but direct *experience* will never distance you from the truth.

Popularity is not a reliable indicator of goodness, truth, or beauty.

Knowledge, truth, and wisdom are found by emulating *the great doers*, not by flocking around *the fancy talkers*.

Never accept anything anyone tells you without putting it to the tests of love and logic for yourself.

WHAT IS SUCCESS?

A life well-lived is not the result of a self-serving cost/benefit analysis. A life well-lived is the living expression of your most deeply held values.

The best way to *be* somebody is to do something that matters, no matter how "humble" that something might be.

Your humanity is defined not by what you have or have not, but by what you choose to *do* with what you have—or have not.

There is no greater measure of your humanity than the significance of the battles you choose to fight.

Greatness is measured not by what you get, but by what you give.

You can never accomplish anything worthwhile without love, work, perseverance, and the willingness to suffer for it.

Being influential is far more admirable than being famous.

Your self-respect is infinitely more important than what people think of you.

Having fun is far more important than winning.

It's okay to keep striving for more—as long as "more" is not just the mere accumulation of wealth, fame, and coercive power.

True wealth is not measured by how much stuff you have. True wealth is the opportunity to pursue your dreams on your own terms.

Your humanity is measured by the victory of your noble aspirations over your human frailties.

True wealth is to have those things that money can't buy.

AUTONOMY & COMMUNITY

Love yourself; love others. What higher precept does anyone need to guide them?

Wholeness as a human being is impossible to conceive without your connection with and significance to others.

The best way to *be* somebody is to *matter* to somebody else.

Your life is deeply enriched by enriching the lives of others.

Be neither selfish nor selfless. Be self-interested and interested in others.

Doing what's truly in your own interest is probably also what's best for the whole world. And so you love others best by loving yourself *more*, not less.

You are on the right path when your freedom and autonomy are balanced with an equal measure of responsibility and fellowship.

There is no greater joy than to share your time, treasure, and talents in service to others.

Service to others: the cure for loneliness, boredom, unhappiness, self-doubt, regret, anxiety, disillusionment, resignation, and fear—but that is not why you do it.

FINDING YOURSELF

The reason you fail to achieve a challenging goal is not because you are stupid, lazy, weak, or untalented, not because you are a quitter or procrastinator, and not because you lack discipline or self-control. The real reason is lack of something infinitely higher and deeper: clarity of purpose.

Willpower does not exist. The only way to stop doing things that are bad for you and to start doing things that are good for you is never a matter of superhuman self-control or self-denial, but of self-possession, impassioned by one thing: clarity of purpose.

Clarity of purpose—a master organizer and purifier, with the power to unclutter your heart and mind of the vulgar, petty, and trivial.

Clarity of purpose—a master energizer, with the power to animate the very best parts of you.

Clarity of purpose—the parent of so many precious children:

the courage to risk,

the discipline to show up to work every day,

the integrity to do the right thing when no one is looking,

the humility to say YES to the "small" things that matter and the wisdom to say NO to the "big" things that don't,

the conviction to ignore the critics, cynics, and naysayers,

and the perseverance to keep on trying when things get tough.

You should be so fortunate to be moved by something greater than your own comfort, ease, and safety—possessed by something so compelling that there is no question of pursuing it because it represents the deepest expression of who you truly are, so much so that you cannot imagine life any other way and so deeply that you consider it a privilege to suffer for it.

DOS & DON'TS

No matter the pressure from above, below, left, or right, never do anything stupid, mean, or cowardly.

Never take or accept anything that does not belong to you.

Be the master of—not a slave to—your time, treasure, and talents.

Eat, drink, work, play, dress, speak, and spend with purpose and enjoyment, not ostentation.

Neither be quick to judge or forgive—because none of us is 100 percent guilty, but none of us is 100 percent innocent either.

Have the wisdom to admit your profound ignorance regarding most matters.

When in doubt, have the courage to trust, even at the risk of being betrayed.

Given the chance, most people would rather use their power to do good. Have the courage to give them that chance, even at the risk of being disappointed.

Use your time, treasure, and talents to *connect* with others—not to *compete* with them.

Own your mistakes and make amends to those you've wronged—completely and without blame or excuses.

Stop collecting *things*—and start making memories to cherish and stories worth telling.

Live above the fray of competition, contention, materialism, greed, corruption, militarism, religiosity, partisanship, and patriotism.

Unclutter your life of all possessions, people, pastimes, and pursuits that are not going in the direction you want to go.

Do what makes you feel alive.

Have some fun and do some good.

BEYOND THANKSGIVING

uthentic gratitude is a *verb*, not a mere sentiment.

Nothing really belongs to you—*nothing*. Not your stuff, not your money, not your health, not your talents, not your titles, not your accomplishments, not your family and friends. Even your own body does not belong to you and will eventually abandon you against your will. So when you use the word *my*, let it be a declaration of profound stewardship, not mere possession.

Every gift—of time, health, wealth, safety, knowledge, talent, skill, experience, opportunity, and freedom *demands* something from you.

But this "demand" is no commandment and not some resentful duty. Quite simply, this "demand" is the natural child of perspective: of the realization that your successes have far more to do with your privileged inheritance and good fortune than anything you've accomplished on your own initiative, of the realization that there are so many others who, through no fault of their own, are not equally blessed, of the realization that you *can* give only because you have the good fortune of having something *to* give, of the realization that we who have fared better in the lottery of life have a natural responsibility to those less fortunate, of the realization that the joy of receiving must be reinvested in the joy of giving, of the realization that it's a privilege, not a burden, to share your time, treasure, and talents with others, and of the realization that you have so much more to be grateful for than to be proud of.

INTEGRITY & AUTHENTICITY

It's stressful and exhausting pretending to be something you are not.

Don't be easily disappointed in others. Be far more concerned about disappointing yourself.

Be far more concerned with your character than with your reputation.

Worry about becoming a better version of *you*—not a superior version of somebody else.

Being true to yourself may require you to become unpopular—and to disappoint others along the way.

You're on the right track when you feel neither below nor above anyone else.

Reject all memberships, alliances, and allegiances that are neither good, nor true, nor beautiful.

Never relinquish the responsibility and privilege of setting your own standards.

The only person you need to explain your behavior to is *you*. And so, *you* must always be your toughest critic.

Your big mistakes in life are not typically errors in *logic*. They are more likely to be *moral* errors. You mess up not because you aren't smart enough, but because you are dishonest, petty, conceited, lazy, selfish, self-righteous, and cowardly.

If you can honestly explain your behavior and motives to yourself, you'll feel no need to explain them to others.

What better measure of your freedom and dignity than to do the right thing when nobody's watching?

What better measure of your freedom and dignity than to do the right thing because it's the right thing to do, not because you seek reward or fear punishment—in this life or any other?

Your humanity is measured not by what you think, believe, or feel, but by what you *do*. And not just by *what* you do, but also *how* you do it and *why* you do it.

Imagine yourself: liberated from the stifling grip of obedience and conformity, uninhibited by self-consciousness, undeterred by criticism and unmoved by flattery, unconstrained by tradition and social norms, unmotivated by the trappings of wealth, fame, and coercive power, having no need for permission, approval, or validation, and uncorrupted by ulterior motives,

Imagine yourself master of and slave to no one.

Even if the universe demands nothing from you, you can still demand something of yourself. And you can still demand something of yourself without demanding anything from the universe in return.

Your autonomy is always a threat to the herd that surrounds you and a threat to the powers that be. So, expect to be ostracized and expect some backlash from above, but never stop believing in yourself. Know that you are on a righteous path of responsible freedom that most people never dare to tread.

The only yardstick that matters is your own sense of right and wrong. And your faithfulness to that yardstick is the only thing that can bring you peace.

MATURITY

Growing up is largely the painful process of learning to see what is right before your eyes.

Growing up requires you to do more than carry your own weight.

Growing up requires you to do the right thing because it's the right thing to do—period.

You're a grownup when *your* imperfections bother you more than the imperfections of others.

You grow up when you realize that life is not all about you.

Growing up requires you to come to terms with the imperfections of your parents—by rising above your disappointments and by finding understanding and possible forgiveness.

You're a grownup when you realize that love is not just an exchange of favors.

You're a grownup when you realize that you—
and only you—are responsible for creating
your own meaning, peace, and happiness.

THE POWER OF WORDS

You will learn much and avoid many regrets by having the wisdom and humility to listen first and talk second—if you even need to speak at all.

Just because something is true doesn't mean it needs to be said. Some truths must forever remain unspoken out of kindness and decency.

When you speak from the heart, your words cannot fail to be eloquent.

You contribute so much more to a conversation by being a sincere asker of questions rather than an adroit expresser of opinions, no matter how informed those opinions might be.

Listening is more than just a nice thing to do. Real listening is an act of wisdom, humility, and courage that has the power to heal and to create hope in places where healing and hope did not exist before.

You become the words you use. So you must put the veracity and spirit of everything you read, write, hear, and speak on trial in order to purify your speech of all deceit, conceit, and cowardice.

Words have the power to create or destroy, to inspire or disillusion, to ennoble or corrupt—and thus to spread either joy or misery.

So, what language do you speak? What language do you *want* to speak? Is it the language of contention or peacemaking? Suspicion or trust? Competition or collaboration? Resentment or reconciliation? Victimhood or empowerment? Blame or responsibility? Withdrawal or engagement? Self-righteousness or humility? Scarcity or abundance?

In a phrase, are you speaking the language of resignation or hope?

FAMILY, FRIENDS, & LOVERS

A pleasure shared means so much more than a pleasure enjoyed alone. A victory celebrated together is so much more joyous than a victory celebrated alone. A burden carried together is so much lighter than a burden carried alone.

The humility and courage to say "I don't know," "I'm afraid," "I'm sorry," or "I need help" has the power to tear down the walls that isolate us from each other—giving us the chance to understand and encourage each other—transforming our fears and imperfections from sources of anxiety and isolation into a basis for fellowship, healing, and hope, and inviting us all to laugh together at our common foibles and cry together at our shared sufferings, in other words, to become true friends.

True friends do more than make each other's lives better. True friends make each other better friends—and better human beings— and make the world a better place. And so friendship is both a precious gift and a great responsibility.

True friends never keep score and can touch and go without the need to possess or to be possessed by the other.

Perfect people do not exist. Unless you accept this fact, you will never be happy with who you have in your life.

Anyone who has more answers than questions isn't curious enough, honest enough, or courageous enough to be your true friend.

You can't be lovers with someone who doesn't love you for the thing about yourself that you love the most.

Distance yourself from people you don't respect.

Distance yourself from those who are petty, angry, dishonest, greedy, ungrateful, and vengeful.

Distance yourself from whiners, critics, naysayers, cynics, hypocrites, liars, cheaters, know-it-alls, haters, and moralizers.

Distance yourself from those who gossip and laugh at the misfortunes and shortcomings of others.

And distance yourself from anyone who tries to possess, constrain, or diminish you.

The truer you are, the fewer but truer your friends will be.

Cherish the small circle of those who really care about you. Sing, dance, laugh, and cry together. Show them and tell them you love and appreciate them every chance you get.

PARENTHOOD

Before you and your partner decide to play God by creating new life, make sure that you can answer *why*—not just to yourself and not just to each other, but also to the rest of humanity, and especially to your children when they start to wonder why.

The monumental decision to create a new life—not to be confused with merely "having a baby"—*better be* an emphatic declaration that life matters, that life is going somewhere, and that life—despite its many risks, sufferings, and ultimate death—is still worth living.

Your job is to make your children's lives *better*—not to be confused with *easier*.

Be deeply interested in your children. In doing so, you are going to help them discover *their* talents and passions without imposing any notions of success upon them.

Give your kids the chance to know how good it feels to have *earned* what they have.

Teach your children the things you wish you knew and give them the emotional support you wish you had.

Your kids learn from the example you set, not from the words you speak.

You teach them good manners by *your* politeness.

You teach them to own their mistakes by owning *your* mistakes.

You teach them honesty, responsibility, generosity, and courage by *your* honesty, responsibility, generosity, and courage.

And you teach them how to love by loving them and by loving others.

Teach your kids to be good helpers—by allowing them to help, no matter how much patience it requires of you. Doing so will bring a lifetime of joy to them, to you, and to the whole world.

A major cause of human suffering is that parents are not honest with their children—especially about matters such as money, work, love, sex, drugs, race, marriage, religion, patriotism, and war.

It's your job to break the cycle of ignorance that you inherited from your elders—a cycle of ignorance that your elders most likely inherited from theirs.

Your task is not to teach your kids *what* to think. It's not even your task to teach your kids *how* to think. It's your responsibility to give your kids things to think *about*.

Make sure your kids know and feel deeply that they are loved and valued—and that the world needs them.

Sometimes you love your kids best by yelling at and hugging them at the same time.

Sometimes you need to rescue your kids from dangers they are too young to understand. But, unless they are in such danger, you don't love your kids by *rescuing* them from their mistakes. Neither do you love your kids by *punishing* them for their mistakes. You love your kids by letting them *own* their mistakes.

Your task is to make adults out of your children—by showing them that sometimes they must sacrifice pleasure and accept pain for the sake of higher ends.

Teach your children that they have more than the *permission*—that they have more than the *right*—that they have the sacred *responsibility*—to question everything.

Teach your children that they should never accept what anybody tells them—you included—without putting it to the tests of love and logic for themselves.

THE DIGNITY OF WORK

How can anybody ever be bored or unemployed when there is so much meaningful work to do?

So many beautiful ways to contribute—to bring food, water, shelter, peace, justice, freedom, knowledge, health, comfort, safety, opportunity, joy, hope, and kindness to others.

A meaningful life is largely created by discovering your passions, developing your talents, and finding the kind of work that enables you to express your core values in service to others. Alas, such is no small feat in a market-driven world whose bottom line is not measured by human happiness.

Money isn't everything, but it *is* something. Never underestimate the freedom and power that come from economic self-sufficiency.

Never let anybody tell you that one kind of work is more meaningful or valuable than another.

The value of your work is not measured by how much money you make or how fancy a title you have.

Meaningful work has a knack for connecting you with others, helping you grow, redeeming your sufferings, making you forget your troubles, and opening doors to places you cannot yet imagine.

INFLUENCE

ever underestimate how much power you have to change the world.

Whether you elevate yourself to your highest ideals or lower yourself to your base impulses, you take the whole universe along for the ride.

You're a teacher. It's not a role you can accept or reject. You can only decide what you want others to learn from you when they hear what you say and watch what you do.

You'll have far more success inspiring others to grow by celebrating the best in them, not by criticizing the worst in them.

You change the world most not by convincing others that you have the answers but by being a living example of your most deeply held values.

Your cleverness might *impress* some people, but your authenticity has the power to *move* people.

Everything you do (or not) casts a vote for what exists in the world: every habit, occupation, possession, pastime, and dollar spent, every relationship, membership, and allegiance, every acceptance or rejection, every promise kept or broken, every honesty or pretense, every encouraging or discouraging word, every act of forgiveness or resentment, generosity or greed, compassion or indifference, courage or cowardice, hope or despair.

Be the kind of person that gives other people something to believe in.

Consider it an honor and privilege, not a burden, to have the freedom and opportunity to fix things you did not break, to correct mistakes you did not make, and to heal wounds you did not inflict.

Every sincere and honorable *doing*, no matter how humble, has the power to illuminate reality and speak the truth—to bring comfort, healing, peace, justice, power, and hope to places that even the most impassioned words alone can never penetrate.

JUST SAY YES

The cynic and pessimist in you will never accomplish anything worthwhile. Optimism—even if considered naive, irrational, or foolhardy by others—is essential to all human progress.

Hopes and dreams are so easily crushed by fear, self-doubt, and self-consciousness—so easily crushed by trusting the cynics, critics, and naysayers. But dreams really can, and really do, come true. Never let anybody tell you different.

Large or small, what matters is that your dreams are *your* dreams—dreams that flow naturally from *your* core values and *your* unique endowment of blessings and burdens—not from the expectations of others.

An authentic dream will make you as you make it. It will teach you, give you courage, confidence, and conviction, and reveal talents and virtues you did not know you possessed.

Wealth, fame, and power are not dreams.
They are ambitions.

An authentic dream brings joy not just to you, but also to others.

An authentic dream fulfilled scores a victory not just for you, but for all humanity.

One of the greatest joys in life is to create something good, true, and beautiful that would not exist without you.

At the risk of being declared naive or foolhardy, place your bets on the optimist in you, in that "crazy" person who refuses to accept NO for an answer when they know the answer is YES.

Beware of anyone who makes a virtue of the word "can't"—yourself included.

THE COURAGE TO BE

Life will challenge you with a thousand reasons to become disillusioned and cynical. It may take all the guts you have to keep on caring in a world where greed, fear, and hatred seem to be much stronger forces than love.

The reasons for quitting are often the very same reasons you must keep on trying.

The disappointment of having tried and failed hurts a bit, but that pain is nothing compared to the anguish of never having tried at all.

Your feelings of self-respect largely flow from the integrity, honesty, and courage to say YES when you mean YES—and NO when you mean NO.

Use your time, treasure, and talents to be *in* the world, not to insulate yourself from danger and responsibility.

If you have the courage to push your limits, you'll likely discover that they weren't limits after all.

Don't try to suppress your fears; face them head on and expand your comfort zones.

Expect to dig a few dry wells, make a few mistakes, make a few enemies, lose a few friends, burn a few bridges, and collect a few regrets along the way. It means you've stood for something and taken the risk of being truly alive.

Your hidden talents and virtues will be revealed to you only after you've had the courage to leave the convenient, comfortable, safe, and predictable behind.

Courage leads; competence, confidence, conviction, and credibility follow.

There is no bigger confidence booster than confronting your fears and living to tell the story.

Sometimes courage means being a warrior.

Sometimes courage means being a peacemaker.

Your first success requires you to stick your neck out. Your second success requires the same. So does your third.

Courage is born of something bigger than fear: a thing called LOVE.

Be *humble* enough to do things that are "beneath" you and *audacious* enough to dare things that are "above" you.

Don't be afraid to let the universe know that you exist.

TICK-TOCK, TICK-TOCK

Life never stops happening. Don't let it happen without you.

Shift your attitude from a universe made of *nouns* to a universe made of *verbs* and notice the profound transformation that occurs in your sense of self and sense of others.

You may not be able to control the number of days you have, but you do have some control over the quantity and quality of meaningful moments you create.

Procrastination does not merely ignore problems. It creates new ones called regrets, a potentially irreversible form of unhappiness.

Procrastination is not necessarily a bad thing. Procrastination may be your heart telling you to find something else to care about. If indeed you need to care about something else, what are you waiting for?

Wouldn't it be nice if living *in* the moment was a simple matter of living *for* the moment?

Time is the most precious thing you have;
never let anybody waste it, yourself included.

Time is the most precious thing you have. Don't waste it on things that are not going in the direction you want to go.

Time is the most precious thing you have. Don't squander it on battles that are beneath your freedom and dignity.

Time is the most precious thing you have. So your time is the most precious gift that you can give to someone and the most precious gift that they can give to you.

Life is a lot shorter than you think. Don't waste any heartbeats.

MEDITATIONS ON FAITH

Given our capacity for injustice and cruelty in the name of so many patent falsehoods, the courageous separation of fact from fiction is a deadly serious matter.

Sincere doubt is more than just a *right*. Sincere doubt is a sacred *responsibility* and the only thing that makes sincere belief even possible.

It is not just irrational, but also *unethical* to believe anything without sufficient evidence or defensible moral argument.

Obedience to "authority" is the *least* reliable way to know the truth. Direct experience is the *most* reliable way to know the truth.

Put your beliefs forever on trial—and challenge them with even more vigor than you challenge the beliefs of others.

Before embracing or rejecting any belief or moral stance, ask yourself: "Do I have a vested interest in adopting one position over another?"

Recognize that the truth matters, even if it hurts, that a belief is not made true because it benefits the believer in you, that your body, mind, and spirit are easily hijacked by ulterior motives, that any worldview that demands little of you should be scrutinized with even more skepticism than a worldview that demands much, and that you'll never know what you *really* believe unless those beliefs have been truly tested—by hunger, thirst, fear, poverty, illness, betrayal, injustice, grief, lust, or danger—not to mention the many temptations that come with wealth, fame, and power.

Practice, not profession, is the only defensible measure of any authentic faith.

Authentic prayer can take many forms: honesty, gratitude, generosity, understanding, curiosity, patience, integrity, trust, forgiveness, reconciliation, restitution, perseverance, courage, compassion, and endurance, to name but a few. Mumbling a few words in the vain hope of getting some supernatural agent to do *your* job is not one of them.

It's not enough to merely *believe* something. It's not even enough to believe *in* something. Freedom and dignity demand that you *stand* for something.

Look in the mirror, not up to the heavens, for your salvation. Because the only thing you need to be saved from is your own ignorance, pettiness, laziness, greed, prejudice, cowardice, self-righteousness, and unjustified pride.

Trust your own eyes, ears, and innate moral compass. Such is not the sin of pride but a form of self-respect and the acceptance of deep responsibility.

Beware any "authority" who would hold the adult in you to a lower standard than you would hold yourself.

Authentic faith does not require you to believe in unbelievable things. Authentic faith requires only that you have faith in yourself and in the power of love.

Put your trust in freedom, logic, honesty, gratitude, kindness, creativity, curiosity, friendship, diversity, community, humility, generosity, fair play, thrift, restraint, forgiveness, empathy, responsibility, integrity, justice, courage, compassion, and love—each of these quite capable of standing on its own merits, without belief in the unbelievable and without sanction from any "authority," earthly or divine.

Real faith comes alive the moment you stop *looking for* the answer and start *being* the answer.

You need not *solve* the mystery of life in order to *live* the mystery of life—with passion and purpose—embracing all its joys and sorrows with honesty, gratitude, humility, creativity, generosity, compassion, courage, and love.

That has to be enough—for that is all we know and perhaps all we can *ever* know.

THE POWER OF LOVE

The greatest meaning, peace, and happiness are made possible by having someone (or someones) to care about.

True love is a *verb*, not a mere sentiment.

Your capacity to love is measured by your capacity to suffer *with* and sometimes to suffer *for*.

Love does not always feel pleasant, but it always feels *right*.

Love is being honest when being honest is an act of courage.

Never take away the power of those you love by doing for them that which they can do for themselves.

Love—sometimes the only reason to keep on living after every other hope and happiness has been stripped away from you.

Not every suffering is fixable. Sometimes all we can do is cry together, holding onto each other with all the compassion and courage we can muster.

Love—the recognition that we are all in the same boat, that we are all brothers and sisters, that we are all damaged children in one way or another, and that we all would benefit if we allowed our hopes, fears, virtues, and foibles to unite us in mutual empathy, mutual affection, and shared purpose.

Love—the radical faith and freedom to care about the *whole* world, not just about your family, friends, neighbors, and those who share your race, country, and creed.

Love—the radical faith and freedom to give without keeping score.

Love—the radical faith and freedom to care about those you disagree with, dislike, and fear—and even those who, in their ignorance and anger, would do you harm.

Live your life as if love is as real and as big as it gets—bigger even than the Big Bang—so big and so real that it has the power to marshal the laws of physics in its service.

Love—where better to invest your freedom, faith, and profound ignorance.

A GOOD DEATH

Live every day like *this* life is the only one you've got—because *this* life probably *is* the only one you've got.

Embrace your mortality by living every day with such audacity, passion, and courage that once is enough.

Immortality is not to be found in some supposed afterlife, but in every beautiful thing that will happen in some distant time and place because *you* were here.

So, why are you here?

Just in case you need a little nudge to get busy with your answer, don't forget: life is a lot shorter than you think. Don't waste any heartbeats.

www.ingramcontent.com/pod-product-compliance
Lightning Source LLC
LaVergne TN
LVHW011949060526
838201LV00061B/4264